the Country Friends Collection™

KiDSTUFF

Holly   **Mary Elizabeth**   **Kate**

... knows Skeeter just flushed 4 alphabet blocks down the toilet and can't bear to look.

... just blew up 46 balloons for the third grade penguin races.

... ate Molly's mudpie by mistake.

go fishin'

visit the Library (SHH!)

Bowl

POPCORN & GIANT SIZE

POP X LG.

Matinee Movies are FUN.

attend a Concert with them

Take a Little Nappy-Poo together in a Hammock

check out the bears at THE ZOO

Play Miniature GOLF

Ice Skating is cool

FUN WAYS

TO SPEND TIME WITH

THE KIDS

Star gazing

Go to the Circus

Pack A Picnic and go!

Take a **Dog obedience class** together (on second thought, maybe tennis lessons are a better idea)

Sing silly songs

go **Swimming**

Play a card game

Kate's Best-ever Chocolate Finger Paint

FOR THE BUDDING ARTIST IN ALL OF US — THE TASTIEST FINGER PAINT OF ALL! TRY VANILLA OR BUTTERSCOTCH, TOO....

4-oz. PKG. instant chocolate pudding mix

2 c. milk
white paper

Prepare pudding mix according to package directions. Let the pudding set 'til thick. Paint on white paper with pudding. Let masterpieces dry for several hours.

Paint, Clay and Playdough

the Country friends™ KIDSTUFF STUDIO

PLAY CLAY

Mary Elizabeth's Super-Duper Play Dough

Great-smelling dough ~ perfect birthday party favors!

- 2-½ c. flour
- ½ c. salt
- 1 T. powdered alum
- 2 pkg. unsweetened fruit-flavored drink mix
- 2 T. vegetable oil
- 2 c. boiling water

Mix together flour, salt, alum & drink mix in large mixing bowl. Add oil. Pour boiling water over flour mixture ~ stir until well-combined. Knead dough until smooth. Store in airtight plastic bag or covered container.

Peanut Butter Play Clay

A SAFE & FUN CLAY FOR LITTLE ONES WHO LIKE TO GIVE THEIR ART THE TASTE TEST!

- 1 c. white corn syrup
- 1 c. powdered sugar
- 1 c. powdered milk
- 1 c. creamy peanut butter

Mix together peanut butter, corn syrup & powdered sugar 'til well-combined. Add powdered milk to mix. Knead until smooth.

If dough seems too sticky, add a little more powdered milk. Let kids decorate their creations with chocolate chips, raisins or other edibles.

Holly's Buddy Putty

KIDS LOVE THIS BLOBBY GLOOP!

- 1 c. white glue
- 2-½ c. liquid starch
- food coloring

Mix glue & 1 cup of liquid starch together in mixing bowl. Add a few drops of food coloring. Mix well. Cover bowl ~ let stand overnight. The next day, while stirring slowly, add 1 to 1½ cups more liquid starch until a big blob forms. Pour off any remaining starch. Store in a covered container.

5

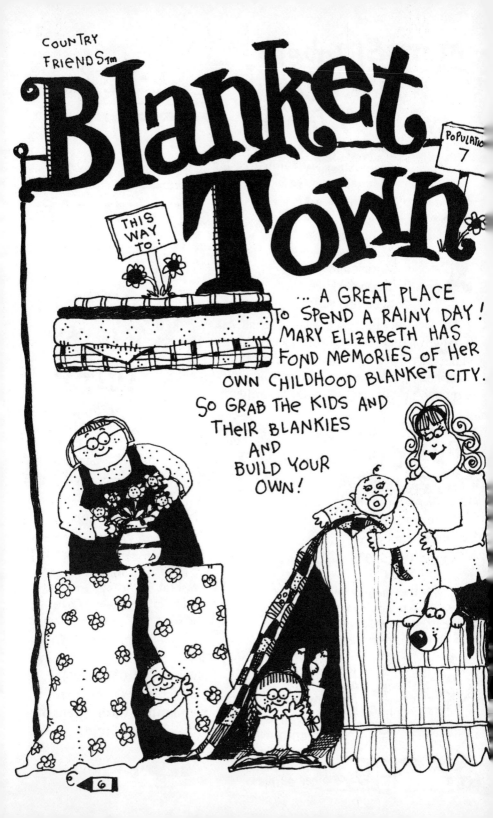

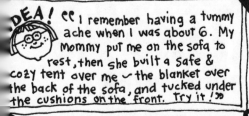

IDEA! "I remember having a tummy ache when I was about 6. My mommy put me on the sofa to rest, then she built a safe & cozy tent over me ~ the blanket over the back of the sofa, and tucked under the cushions on the front. Try it!"

JUST COVER CHAIRS OR A TABLE WITH BLANKETS, QUILTS OR SHEETS TO FORM A TENT. LET KIDS BE CREATIVE BY COMBINING CHAIRS WITH TABLE TO BUILD A BIGGER TENT ~ JUST BE SURE THAT THE CHAIRS ARE CAPABLE OF HOLDING HEAVY BLANKETS!

MAKE THE TENTS
COZY and **FUN**
WITH STUFF LIKE:

PILLOWS
FLASHLIGHTS
SLEEPING BAGS
GAMES
TOM SAWYER BOOKS
TOYS
SNACKS

KATE'S BLANKET TOWN TORTILLA TREATS

A PERFECT SNACK FOR YOUR HUNGRY YOUNG BUILDERS!

INGREDIENTS:
- FLOUR TORTILLAS
- PEANUT BUTTER
- MINI CHOCOLATE CHIPS

HOW TO:

SIMPLY SPREAD THE PEANUT BUTTER ON THE OPEN TORTILLA.

SPRINKLE CHOCOLATE CHIPS ON THE PEANUT BUTTER, THEN ROLL UP THE TORTILLA.

SCRUMPTIOUS!

KATE'S CAVE
NO ADMITTANCE

7

BALLOON BUFFOONERY

KEEP A BAG O' BALLOONS ON HAND FOR ALL KINDS OF REVELRY!

BALLOON SOCCER

HIT THE BALLOON AROUND USING YOUR HEAD, KNEES & ELBOWS
NO FAIR USING HANDS & FEET!

INDOOR VOLLEY-BALLOON CHALLENGE

Make a net by tying a string or two between 2 chairs. (For pre-schoolers, lay a bright yarn string on the floor for a net.)

Children can use their hands to bat the balloon back & forth over the net. To score a point, the balloon must hit the floor on the opposing player's side of the net. Points may also be scored when it takes more than 3 tries to get the balloon over the net.

WATER BALLOON BUST

GREAT FUN OUTSIDE ON A HOT SUMMER DAY!

Fill balloons with water and tie closed. Grab a partner! Toss water-filled balloon back & forth, increasing distance apart with each throw until···· **OO**PS! the balloon breaks!

* Be sure to pick up broken pieces of balloons ∽ they can be very hazardous to small children & pets.

GAMES & FUN

PENGUIN RACE
....GIGGLES GALORE!

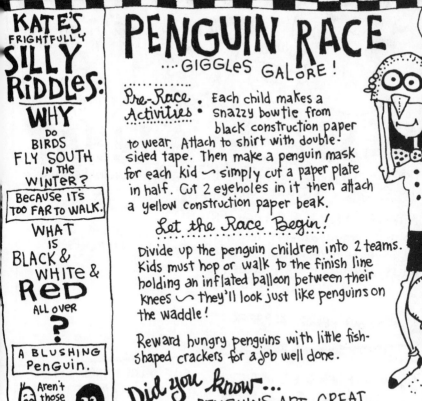

Pre-Race Activities • Each child makes a snazzy bowtie from black construction paper to wear. Attach to shirt with double-sided tape. Then make a penguin mask for each kid ⌐ simply cut a paper plate in half. Cut 2 eyeholes in it then attach a yellow construction paper beak.

Let the Race Begin!

Divide up the penguin children into 2 teams. Kids must hop or walk to the finish line holding an inflated balloon between their knees ⌐ they'll look just like penguins on the waddle!

Reward hungry penguins with little fish-shaped crackers for a job well done.

Did you know...

PENGUINS ARE GREAT JUMPERS? THEY CAN LEAP AS HIGH AS **8** FEET OUT OF WATER TO LAND ON THE SHORE!

BOING!

snow games

TIC☆TAC☆SNOW

MAKE A TIC-TAC-TOE BOARD IN THE SNOW WITH FOOTPRINTS. PLAYERS HOP FROM SQUARE-TO-SQUARE TO MAKE X's & O's.

RAINBOW SNOW ☆

REMIND KIDS TO SQUIRT <u>ONLY</u> SNOW OR YOU'LL END UP WITH RAINBOW KIDS & CLOTHES!

- WATER
- FOOD COLORING
- SQUIRT GUNS OR BOTTLES WITH SQUIRT SPOUTS

FILL SQUIRT GUNS & BOTTLES WITH WATER. ADD FOOD COLORING TO EACH BOTTLE & GUN. SHAKE TO MIX. SQUIRT COLOR ON SNOWMEN, SNOW ANGELS & SNOWFORTS ⌐ MAKE COLORFUL DESIGNS IN THE SNOW!

GUESS ? WHAT

A FUN-BUT-MEMORY-BENDING-GAME TO PLAY WITH FRIENDS!

WHAT YOU NEED

- A PAPER & PENCIL FOR EACH FRIEND
- 10 TO 20 SMALL OBJECTS THAT FIT INTO HANDS, SUCH AS BUTTONS, COINS, PEANUTS IN THE SHELL, WRAPPED CANDY, PAPERCLIPS, BALLS, CRAYONS, RUBBERBANDS, ETC.

HOW TO PLAY

1. PASS OUT PENCIL & PAPER.

2. CHOOSE SOMEONE TO BE SCOREKEEPER.

3. HAVE FRIENDS SIT IN A TIGHT CIRCLE WITH HANDS BEHIND THEIR BACKS. SCOREKEEPER WILL PLACE AN OBJECT IN THE HANDS OF ONE OF THE PLAYERS WITHOUT LETTING ANYONE SEE THE OBJECT. THAT PLAYER PASSES IT SECRETLY TO THE NEXT PERSON AND SO ON UNTIL IT HAS GONE COMPLETELY AROUND THE CIRCLE.

4. SCOREKEEPER KEEPS PLACING OBJECTS INTO THE HANDS OF THE FIRST PLAYER. THAT PLAYER KEEPS PASSING THEM ON WITH SCOREKEEPER COLLECTING OBJECTS FROM THE LAST PLAYER.

5. AFTER THE LAST OBJECT IS PASSED AROUND THE CIRCLE, PLAYERS MUST WRITE DOWN IN ORDER ALL OBJECTS THAT WERE PASSED. THE WINNER IS THE PLAYER WITH THE MOST CORRECT ANSWERS!

The great man is he who does not lose his child's-heart. —Mencius

Nutty about Nature!

Grab the kids and Go for a walk!

It's fun...

Hike around the neighborhood, a park, the local lake, a country road or an indoor botanical garden.

Look at all the things around you — take time to sit in the grass, smell the flowers, feel the breeze.

Kids love to bring home nature's souvenirs like stones, leaves & sticks. Use them in these Country Friend™ projects....

Still young at heart, just a little tired in the legs.

MOM

Painted rocks make wonderful paperweights for Mom or Dad's desk... add a name for a very special personalization!

ROCKS & STONES

Can be turned into special creatures with a dab of paint & a dot of glue! Be creative, kids!

FROSTY   ELVIS

FeatHers

are especially intriguing to children — take a moment to appreciate the beauty of a feather you find on your hike. Show your kids the wonderful colors, designs & textures on a feather.

Different ones look beautiful tucked into a wreath or vase, or try your hand at painting with a feather!

How **Interesting**:

★Did you know a Robin has almost **3000 feathers?**

STicks

can be gathered up and painted with acrylics — a fun project on a winter afternoon! Paint some solid colors, some polka-dotted, some striped. Display in a jar or vase for a unique table decoration.

Some sticks look like animals or snakes — paint 'em in bright colors and add eyes!

Spraypaint sticks white & dust with clear glitter for a pretty winter display.

Leaves

make interesting rubbings and look wonderful framed for wall decor. Set leaves face down on a table and cover with a sheet of light-colored paper ~ fresh, un-crinkly leaves work best. With a wax crayon, gently rub the paper until the image of a leaf appears. Pieces of tree bark also make pretty rubbings ~ but remember, never take bark off a living tree! Just use pieces you've found on the ground.

Nature stamps

YOU WILL NEED:

- SEASONED BLOCKS OF WOOD (FROM A LUMBERYARD)
- INTERESTING-SHAPED LEAVES, GRASSES & TWIGS
- GLUE
- PAINT
- PAINT BRUSHES & SMALL PAINT ROLLER

1. On one side of block of wood, glue a leaf and several pieces of grass or twigs.

2. With a paintbrush or roller, apply paint to raised design. Press onto piece of scrap paper to "test" your design.

3. Use your nature stamp to print pretty stationery, wrapping paper or unique wall borders.

Snow

only adds to the fun of a hike! Pull on your mittens and take a snow trek.

Take note of creatures' tracks in the snow ~ try and guess who those little prints belong to, and imagine where they lead!

And on your way home, pack a few snowballs in your parka pockets ~ stash 'em in the freezer for the hottest July afternoon!

A Secret Message

Hmmmm....

Make a Top-Secret Code using numbers & letters (we've, uh, borrowed Kate's Secret Code — see chart at left) and send a message out using country friends™ Invisible Ink.

A	1
B	2
C	3
D	4
E	5
F	6
G	7
H	8
I	9
J	10
K	11
L	12
M	13
N	14
O	15
P	16
Q	17
R	18
S	19
T	20
U	21
V	22
W	23
X	24
Y	25
Z	26

★ Lemon Juice
★ Round Toothpick
★ White Paper such as typing paper
★ Lamp with at least a 75-watt bulb

Dip one end of toothpick in lemon juice (also known to secret agents as invisible ink).

Write message on white paper with end of the toothpick that has been dipped in invisible ink. You'll need to dip several times as you write your message.

Let dry.

Send secret message to a friend who knows the secret code. To read it, hold paper over a hot lightbulb until lemon juice letters turn brown. (Moms — help junior agents with this step. Don't let hands or paper touch the hot bulb!)

— — — — — — — — — — — — — .

25 15 21   1 18 5   13 25 2 5 19 20   6 18 9 5 14 4

Decode It!

14

Lightning Bug Tag

A VERSION OF FLASHLIGHT TAG ~ FUN ON A DARK SUMMER NIGHT!

1 GATHER PLAYERS TOGETHER WHEN IT'S DARK OUTSIDE. CHOOSE A PLAYER TO BE THE LIGHTNING BUG. THIS PLAYER GETS TO CARRY THE FLASHLIGHT.

2 DESIGNATE HOME BASE. THE LIGHTNING BUG COUNTS <u>SLOWLY</u> TO 50 WITH EYES CLOSED & FLASHLIGHT OFF SO PLAYERS CAN HIDE.

☆ ADVICE TO PARENTS: MARK OFF A SAFE AREA, FREE FROM DANGER, FOR THE GAME TO BE PLAYED IN, AND LET KIDS KNOW WHERE THE BOUNDARIES ARE FOR PLAY.

ME! ME! CHOOSE ME! ME! OK? ME?

NO PEEKING, NOW.

3 THE LIGHTNING BUG TURNS ON THE FLASHLIGHT AND SEARCHES FOR THE OTHER PLAYERS. TO ESCAPE BEING CAPTURED BY THE LIGHTNING BUG, PLAYERS MUST MAKE IT FROM THEIR HIDING PLACE TO HOME BASE WITHOUT BEING TAGGED BY THE FLASHLIGHT BEAM.

4 THE PLAYER TAGGED FIRST BY THE FLASHLIGHT BECOMES THE LIGHTNING BUG.

GOTCHA!

Backward, turn backward, O time, in your flight make me a child again just for tonight! ~ Elizabeth Akers Allen

15

SPOTTY THE Great and his INCREDIBLE ICE CUBE TRICK

Pick up an ice cube without even touching it with your bare paws, er, hands!

FOR THIS ASTOUNDING FEAT, YOU'LL NEED:

* COTTON STRING
* ICE CUBE
* WATER
* MAGIC CRYSTALS (SALT)

THE SECRET HOW-TO:

Place string in water until it is completely soaked. Suspend one end of the string over the ice cube until it touches the top of the ice cube and remains there. Sprinkle some Magic Crystals on the ice cube. Slowly count to 10. Be sure to keep the string on top of the cube. Lift the ice cube up with the string.

SPOTERONI and the BEWILDERING RUBBER BONES

* THIS TRICK IS RECOMMENDED FOR KIDS OVER AGE 6.

Test YOUR super~powers! Are you as strong as the bones?

YOU WILL NEED:

* BONES: CHICKEN LEGS OR WISHBONES WORK GREAT
* WATER
* BLEACH
* GLASS JAR
* VINEGAR

1. Save bones from supper. Wash in water. 2. With an adult's help, put bones in glass jar with 2 cups water & ¼ cup bleach. Cover jar~let sit for at least 1 day. 3. Remove from jar and wash bones with water with adult's help. Let adult dispose of bleach solution. 4. Fill clean jar 3/4 full of vinegar and add bones. Make sure they're covered! Cover jar with tight lid. Leave in jar at least 5 days. Take bone out~ rinse with water. Bones should be bendable. If not, return to jar for a few more days. 5. Try to break the bones!

an amazing trick for budding magicians!

THE **AMAZING SPOTINI** and his ASTONISHING **FLOATING RAISINS**

GATHER THESE SECRET INGREDIENTS :
- GLASS OF WATER
- BAKING SODA
- 4 TO 6 RAISINS (PLUS SOME EXTRAS TO SNACK ON!)
- VINEGAR

1. Fill glass about 3/4 full of water ~ don't fill completely full.
2. Stir in 1 tablespoon of baking soda until completely dissolved and water has turned clear again.
3. Drop in raisins. They should sink to bottom of the glass.
4. Pour in 2 to 5 tablespoons of vinegar. Say several magic words ~ RISE RAISINS, RISE! Shazamm! MAGICAL!

...and now, for my final trick, I shall make a **SUNNY DAY FLOAT!**

- 6-OZ. CAN FROZEN ORANGE JUICE
- VANILLA ICE CREAM

PREPARE JUICE ACCORDING TO PACKAGE DIRECTIONS. PUT A SCOOP OF ICE CREAM IN EACH GLASS. FILL WITH JUICE. SERVE WITH STRAW & SPOON ~ WATCH IT MAGICALLY DISAPPEAR!

17

...Pretty good tricks for somebody who can't even roll over.

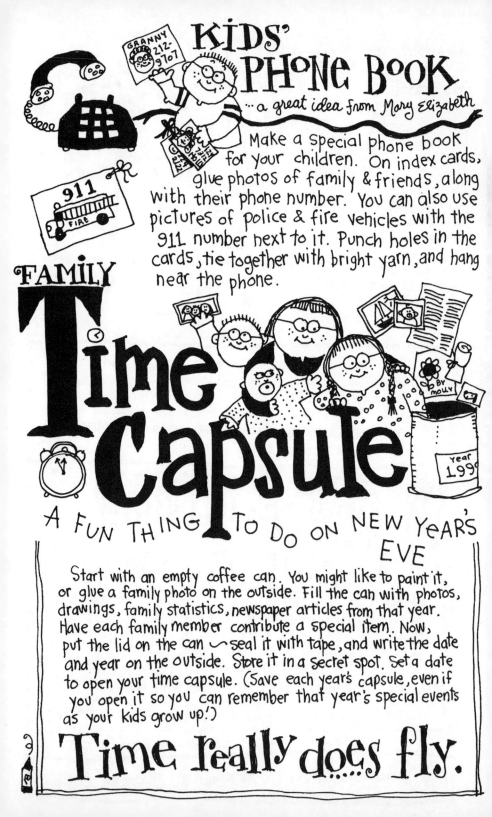

KIDS' PHONE BOOK

...a great idea from Mary Elizabeth

GRANNY 212-9707

Make a special phone book for your children. On index cards, glue photos of family & friends, along with their phone number. You can also use pictures of police & fire vehicles with the 911 number next to it. Punch holes in the cards, tie together with bright yarn, and hang near the phone.

911 FIRE

FAMILY Time Capsule

BY MOLLY

Year 1999

A FUN THING TO DO ON NEW YEAR'S EVE

Start with an empty coffee can. You might like to paint it, or glue a family photo on the outside. Fill the can with photos, drawings, family statistics, newspaper articles from that year. Have each family member contribute a special item. Now, put the lid on the can ⌣ seal it with tape, and write the date and year on the outside. Store it in a secret spot. Set a date to open your time capsule. (Save each year's capsule, even if you open it so you can remember that year's special events as your kids grow up!)

Time really does fly.

AQUANOCULARS

View underwater creatures with these easy-to-make water binoculars!

YOU WILL NEED:

- (2) 12 oz. plastic foam or paper cups
- Heavy-Duty clear plastic wrap
- (2) Small rubber bands & (1) Large rubber band

1. Remove the bottom from each of the cups.
2. Cut 2 pieces of plastic wrap so they will cover the bottoms & sides of each cup.
3. Secure with small rubber bands.
4. Using the large rubber band, fasten the 2 cups together.
5. In shallow water, tip the aquanoculars slightly as you slip them into the water to prevent an air bubble from being trapped between plastic & the water. Don't let water get into the cup.

The pressure of the water causes it to work almost like a magnifying lens. Many of the plants & animals will seem larger than they really are.

HOW'S THE VIEW?

I saw the biggest feet I ever did see!

I saw all sorts of neat moss and rocks on the bottom!

I saw the LOCH NESS MONSTER! I DID! I REALLY DID!

Take a set on YOUR next underwater expedition!

19

Magic Bubble Wands

About

Collections

HOLLY REMEMBERS:

I loved collecting teddy bears as a girl... and I still do. Begin a collection for your child ~anything will do, as long as your child is interested and it is affordable!

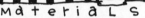

Materials:

* BELL WIRE (FOUND AT HARDWARE STORES)
* 3" COOKIE CUTTERS
* DOWEL ROD
* DRILL
* GLUE

Leaving a 1-½" tail of wire on each end, wrap bell wire around cookie cutter until ends meet to form the shape for the wand. Twist tail ends together to secure shape. Remove wire shape from cookie cutter.

Drill a small hole in one end of the dowel rod. Fill with a dab of glue~ insert twisted wire ends in hole. Let dry.

Dip wand into Super Bubbles ~ pucker up and

blow a bubble!

Some Ideas:

BILL — BASEBALL CARDS
OLD KEYS
STAMPS
LEAVES
DOLLS
CHRISTMAS ORNAMENTS
MODEL CARS
SHELLS
ANIMAL FIGURINES
CHARMS
BUTTERFLIES
BUGS!
Raggedy Ann Stories
HATS
PENCILS
BOOKS
SNOWGLOBES
FLAGS
COINS
ANGELS

What a difference it makes to come home to a child!

~MARGARET FULLER

How does my Garden Grow?

Kids **Love** to get dirty; gardening is a great way to learn and get dirty at the same time!

GROW A POTATO VINE

YOU NEED:
- POTATO, WHITE OR SWEET VARIETY
- CLEAN GLASS JAR
- ROUND TOOTHPICKS
- WATER

PLACE POTATO IN JAR — DON'T CLEAN OR PEEL. WATER SHOULD TOUCH ONLY BOTTOM OF POTATO. USE TOOTHPICKS TO HOLD POTATO UP IN JAR. PLACE IN SUNNY SPOT. CHANGE WATER ON A WEEKLY BASIS BUT BE SURE WATER IS ALWAYS TOUCHING BOTTOM OF THE POTATO.

MUD PIES

GOOD "CLEAN" FUN FOR LITTLE KIDS & BABIES!

- DIRT
- WATER
- BIG TUB
- EMPTY ALUMINUM PIE TINS OR PAPER PLATES
- PIE "DECORATIONS" SUCH AS FLOWERS, TWIGS, FEATHERS, GRASS & LEAVES

MIX DIRT & WATER IN THE TUB. GIVE KIDS PIE PANS OR PLATES. LET 'EM DIG IN, SO TO SPEAK! THEY CAN DECORATE THEIR PIES WITH TWIGS, ETC., & LET PIES "BAKE" IN THE SUN.
(Have your camera ready!)

Indoor Gardening

FOR PLENTY O' FUN YEAR-ROUND!

Select easy-to-care-for plants like ivy, Boston Fern, corn plant, Wandering Jew, Spider plants or Philodendron.

As your plant grows, you'll need to give it a new, roomier home...

REPOT IT!

1. Select a slightly larger pot than the current one. Put a layer of stones, pebbles or broken pieces of a clay pot in the bottom.

2. Fill pot halfway with good quality potting soil.

3. Gently remove plant from small pot. Carefully brush away some of the soil from around the roots. Put in new pot—add more soil & water well!

A LITTLE DIRT WON'T HURT.

KIDS LOVE A Butterfly Garden

... PLANT THESE IN A SMALL PLOT TO ATTRACT ALL KINDS OF "WINGED FAIRIES": PINEAPPLE SAGE, LAVENDER, NICOTIANA, HYSSOP, CORAL BELLS.

Scratch your name or a message in the soft skin of a growing pumpkin with a nail—when it matures, you'll have a personalized pumpkin!

PUMPKIN PATCH

YOU DON'T HAVE TO LIVE IN THE COUNTRY TO HAVE YOUR VERY OWN PATCH!

- PUMPKIN SEEDS FOR MINIATURE VARIETIES SUCH AS "JACK BE LITTLE"
- LARGE POT
- SOIL

PLANT SEEDS IN SOIL IN LARGE POT. PLACE ON DECK OR PATIO IN A SUNNY SPOT. DON'T FORGET TO WATER! YOUR CROP OF "JACK BE LITTLES" MAKE GREAT PIES, AND LOOK CUTE IN FALL ARRANGEMENTS, TOO.

23

PLaNT peopLe

...FUN LITTLE INDOOR GARDENS FOR KIDS!

- empty eggshell or a large potato
- cotton balls
- markers
- buttons
- straight pins
- grass, alfalfa or radish seeds

If using an empty eggshell, try to make sure only about ¼" of the top has been removed. Rinse with water. The potato needs to have the top removed also. Using a spoon, scoop out a 1"-deep hole in the potato. Stand eggshell up in egg cup or place potato in a small bowl with the scooped-out end on top. Put cotton balls inside egg or in potato hole. Sprinkle with water.

Sprinkle seeds over damp cotton balls. Using marker, draw face on eggshell. Use pins to attach buttons to potato for eyes. Place in a sunny spot and in a few days, you'll have a crop of hairy friends!

24

WORM FARM

EEEEEK! A WORM!

DON'T BE AFRAID OF THE HUMBLE EARTHWORM; IT'S ONE OF THE MOST IMPORTANT THINGS YOU CAN ADD TO YOUR GARDEN. KIDS CAN GROW A WORM FARM UNDER THE KITCHEN SINK OR IN A DARK CLOSET ⁓ THEY MAKE GOOD PETS. THEY'RE QUIET, WON'T CHEW UP YOUR SLIPPERS, AND THEY'LL EAT FRUIT & VEGGIE TABLE SCRAPS!

You'll Need:

- A PLASTIC CONTAINER WITH LID, 10-12" DEEP
- AWL OR NAIL
- SHREDDED NEWSPAPER
- 4-5 c. SOIL
- BUNCH OF EARTHWORMS
- WATER
- MOIST KITCHEN SCRAPS

#1. USING AWL OR NAIL, POKE A FEW AIR HOLES IN UPPER PART OF CONTAINER.

#2. PLACE A HANDFUL OF SHREDDED NEWSPAPER IN CONTAINER. MIX IN SOIL. SPRINKLE WITH ½ c. WATER ⁓ TOSS.

#3. NOW PUT WORMS IN CONTAINER ⁓ WATCH 'EM DIG IN!

#4. ADD MOIST KITCHEN SCRAPS LIKE LEFTOVER DINNER VEGGIES OR APPLE OR POTATO PEELINGS ⁓ ANYTHING WILL WORK AS LONG AS IT'S NOT TOO MUSHY.

INTERESTING WORM FACTS

Earthworms have neither eyes nor ears ⁓ they are sensitive to light & touch by means of sensory cells.

Some earthworms have as many as 10 hearts.

There are earthworms as short as ⅟₂₅ of an inch, and as long as 11 feet!

#5. YOUR WORMS ARE TURNING THE NEWSPAPER & SCRAPS INTO COMPOST. REMOVE SOME COMPOST & MIX IT WITH YOUR GARDEN SOIL OR HOUSEPLANTS. BE SURE TO REPLACE NEWSPAPER & SOIL PERIODICALLY, AND FEED YOUR LITTLE BUDDIES MORE TABLE SCRAPS EVERY OTHER DAY. PUT WORMS IN GARDEN WHEN YOUR PROJECT ENDS.

Worm

25

Let's Get Cooking!

KITCHEN GLOSSARY

Blend – to mix ingredients together until they are smooth.

Cream – to combine sugar & fat together 'til the mixture is smooth & creamy.

Beat – to mix very fast with a spoon or beater to make ingredients fluffy, light or smooth.

Stir – mixing with a circular motion.

Sift – putting dry ingredients like flour through a sieve or screen.

Chop – cut into small pieces.

Bake – to cook in an oven.

Melt – heat until a solid becomes a liquid.

Mary Elizabeth's Kids' Cooking School

Remedial Cooking Class

JR. CHEF

JR. CHEF

BAKING CAKES
PIES
COOKIES

...The Kitchen, the house's warm Heart. – anne Rivers Siddon

FiRST OF ALL, SeT SOME Kitchen RULES:

1. Hair neat & out of the way.
Hair ✓net ✓CAP ✓Space Helmet

2. ALWaYs wash hands before preparing food.
SOAP →

3. Wear an APRON to keep clothes neat and CLEAN.

4. ASK permission to use the kitchen.
May I?

5. Be sure the work area is Clean before & after you use the kitchen.

6. Use different SPOONS for STIRRING and TASTING!

7. Be careful When handling sharp knives! Carry the knife point down ∽ cut away from you ∽ protect counters with a cutting board.

8. Turn pan handles INWARD on the stove so they won't be knocked over or pulled off the stove.

9. Use some POT-Holders or oven mitts when handling hot pans or removing baked goods from the oven.

10. Keep cookbooks, potholders, <u>anything</u> flammable <u>away</u> from **the STOVE.**
Pies

YUMMY STUFF

KIDS LOVE TO FIX

THE BIGGEST KID OF ALL!

Kate's Seal of Approval

PIZZA COBBLER

~ an easy and delicious snack!

- PIZZA SAUCE
- 1 CAN REFRIGERATOR BISCUITS
- 1-⅓ c. MOZZARELLA cheese, SHREDDED

GREASE AN 8-INCH SQUARE PAN WITH VEGETABLE OIL SPRAY. PLACE ABOUT ¼ OF THE PIZZA SAUCE IN BOTTOM OF THE PAN. CUT EACH BISCUIT IN 4 PIECES. ROLL BISCUIT PIECES INTO BALLS AND PLACE IN PAN ON TOP OF SAUCE. POUR REMAINING SAUCE OVER BISCUITS. SPRINKLE WITH MOZZARELLA CHEESE. BAKE IN 400° OVEN FOR 15 TO 20 MINUTES. ENJOY!

CINNAMON TOAST

- 1-½ t. CINNAMON
- 2 T. SUGAR
- 4 SLICES BREAD
- BUTTER OR MARGARINE

MIX CINNAMON & SUGAR. TOAST BREAD & SPREAD WITH BUTTER. SPRINKLE WITH CINNAMON & SUGAR MIX.

A boy is an appetite with a skin pulled over it.
— anonymous

all our favorite ingredients are in my

MOLLY

Nutty COCOA

~ peanut butter, chocolate and marshmallows!

- 4 c. MILK
- ½ c. CHOCOLATE-FLAVORED DRINK MIX
- ¼ c. CREAMY PEANUT BUTTER
- ½ t. VANILLA
- MINIATURE MARSHMALLOWS

IN A SAUCEPAN, COMBINE CHOCOLATE MIX WITH 1-½ c. MILK UNTIL WELL-BLENDED. MIX IN PEANUT BUTTER, AND ADD REMAINING MILK. HEAT COCOA 'TIL ALMOST BOILING. POUR INTO MUGS AND TOP WITH MARSHMALLOWS.

YUM

EASY Recipes

IS IT MORE FUN TO MAKE IT OR EAT IT?

RAINBOW Toast

- BREAD
- FOOD COLORING
- CLEAN PAINTBRUSHES OR COTTON SWABS

PLACE 4 DROPS OF FOOD COLORING IN EACH SECTION OF A MUFFIN TIN. ADD 1 TO 2 T. WATER TO DILUTE COLORS. DIP PAINTBRUSH INTO FOOD COLORING AND PAINT DESIGNS ON BREAD. PLACE IN TOASTER AND TOAST. BUTTER & EAT IT UP!

Old-fashioned CANDLE SALAD

~ a fun fruit salad for kids to make for a holiday dinner!

- BIBB LETTUCE LEAVES
- CANNED PINEAPPLE RINGS
- BANANAS
- WHIPPED TOPPING
- MARASCHINO CHERRIES

PLACE ONE LETTUCE LEAF ON EACH PLATE. LAY A PINEAPPLE SLICE ON TOP OF LETTUCE. CUT BANANA IN HALF AND STAND IN HOLE OF EACH PINEAPPLE RING. TOP EACH BANANA WITH A DAB OF WHIPPED TOPPING ~ PUT CHERRY ON TOP OF WHIPPED TOPPING. Beautiful!

HUH??

DOG & SOUP Lunch

...a warm & delicious school lunch, brown-bag style!

- HOT DOG, COOKED (RELAX, SPOTTY!)
- YOUR CHILD'S FAVORITE SOUP ~ ALPHABET, VEGGIE OR CREAM OF TOMATO WORKS GREAT
- HOT DOG BUN

TIE A STRING AROUND THE COOKED HOT DOG. PLACE HOT DOG IN A THERMOS WITH STRING HANGING OUT OVER THE SIDE ~ THAT'S HOW THE KID WILL RETRIEVE THE HOT DOG! POUR HOT SOUP INTO THERMOS OVER HOT DOG AND SEAL WITH THERMOS LID. WRAP HOT DOG BUN IN PLASTIC WRAP TO ROUND OUT THE MEAL. (OF COURSE, DON'T FORGET TO ADD SOME COOKIES IN THE LUNCH BAG, TOO)

When I was at home, I was in a better Place.

~ WM. SHAKESPEARE ~

Navajo Fry Bread

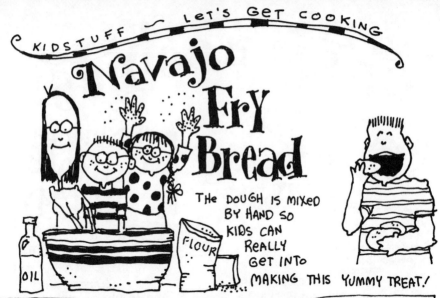

THE DOUGH IS MIXED BY HAND SO KIDS CAN REALLY GET INTO MAKING THIS YUMMY TREAT!

★ Parents will want to supervise the frying process. ★

- 4 c. FLOUR
- 1 T. BAKING POWDER
- 1 t. SALT
- 2 T. DRY MILK POWDER
- 1·½ c. WARM WATER
- 1 c. COOKING OIL

MIX TOGETHER FLOUR, BAKING POWDER, SALT & DRY MILK IN A LARGE BOWL. POUR IN WATER. MIX WITH YOUR HANDS UNTIL A SOFT DOUGH HAS BEEN FORMED. PULL OFF A SMALL PORTION OF DOUGH ~ ABOUT 2 TABLESPOONS WORTH. POUND & PULL DOUGH UNTIL IT IS FLAT & ROUND. HEAT COOKING OIL IN A SKILLET. FRY BREAD DOUGH IN HOT OIL UNTIL IT IS GOLDEN BROWN ON EACH SIDE. REMOVE BREAD ~ DRAIN ON PAPER TOWEL. SPRINKLE WITH HONEY, CINNAMON & SUGAR, JELLY OR A FAVORITE TACO FILLING ~ YUM!

The best smell is bread.
The best savor salt.
The best love that of Children.

~ old proverb ~

30

Creepy Crawly FUN

Kids are always fascinated with magnets ...and creepy crawly things!

- CONSTRUCTION PAPER
- CRAYONS, MARKERS, COLORED PENCILS
- SCISSORS
- PAPER FASTENERS (SOME ARE NOT ATTRACTED BY MAGNETS SO CHECK BEFORE BUYING!)
- SMALL MAGNET
- PAPER PLATE

1. ON CONSTRUCTION PAPER, LET KIDS DESIGN THEIR FAVORITE BUG, LIZARD, SNAKE OR CREEPY CRAWLY USING CRAYONS, MARKERS OR PENCILS. DESIGNS SHOULD BE SMALL ENOUGH TO FIT ON THE PAPER PLATES. CUT DESIGN OUT WITH SCISSORS.

2. INSERT PAPER FASTENERS TO FORM LEGS OR ANTENNAE ON CREEPY CRAWLIES.

3. DRAW FOOD, LEAVES, BUGGY HOMES OR EVEN A CREEPY CRAWLY MAZE ON THE PAPER PLATE WITH PENCILS OR MARKERS.

4. PLACE YOUR CREATURES ON PLATE. TO MAKE THEM MOVE, PLACE MAGNET UNDERNEATH THE PLATE AND MOVE AROUND... WATCH 'EM RUN!

Children are a poor man's riches.
—THOMAS FULLER—

QUACK CUP

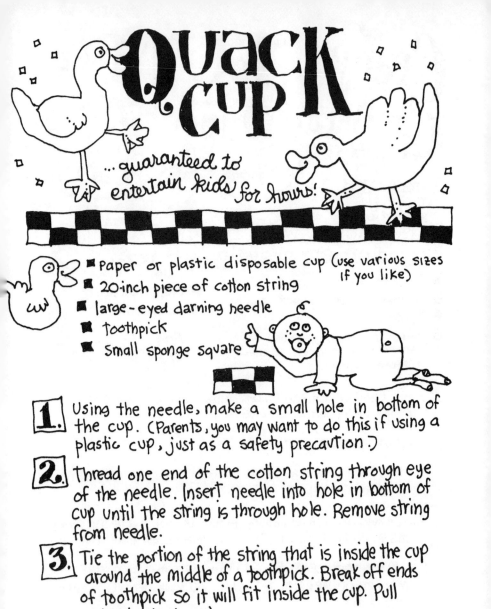

...guaranteed to entertain kids for hours!

- Paper or plastic disposable cup (use various sizes if you like)
- 20-inch piece of cotton string
- large-eyed darning needle
- toothpick
- small sponge square

1. Using the needle, make a small hole in bottom of the cup. (Parents, you may want to do this if using a plastic cup, just as a safety precaution.)

2. Thread one end of the cotton string through eye of the needle. Insert needle into hole in bottom of cup until the string is through hole. Remove string from needle.

3. Tie the portion of the string that is inside the cup around the middle of a toothpick. Break off ends of toothpick so it will fit inside the cup. Pull string back through.

4. Wet the sponge square. Press wet sponge around cotton string. Hold tight — pull away from cup!

QUACK! QUACK!

31